HOW TO HAVE

SELF-CONFIDENCE

COMPLETE GUIDE FOR KIDS

10 YEARS AND UP

BY **HELGA RAY**

Original version: French

CONTENTS

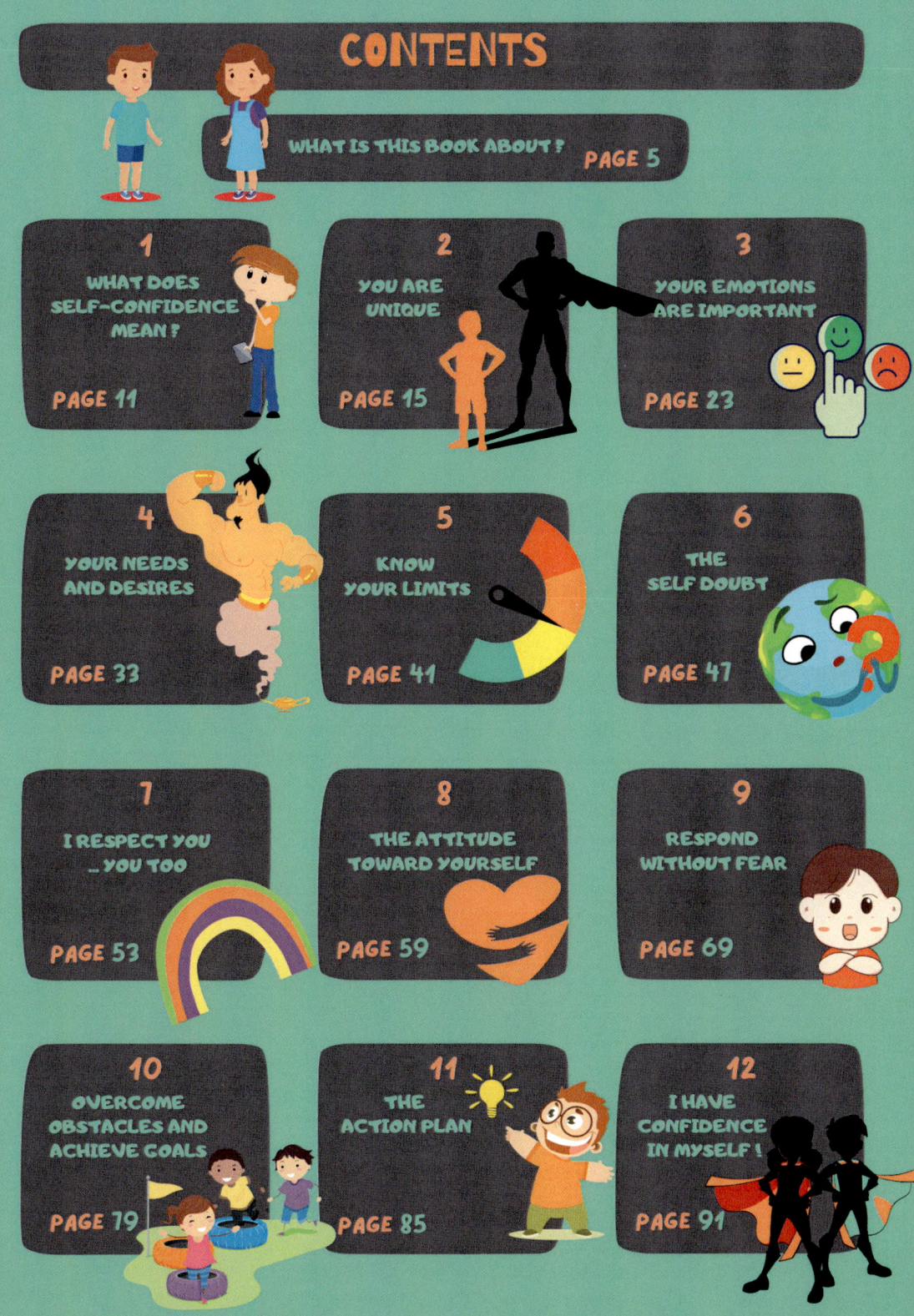

What is this book about?

WHAT IS THIS BOOK ABOUT ?

In this book, I will explain to you how to live situations without losing self-confidence and even how to regain self-confidence.

It often happens in life to be sensitive, to not feel important enough or strong enough to get through. Someone may have made a bad comment, or maybe a joke about you. Or a friend replied to you with a frown.

1

Pay attention to the colors of the book; there is a lot of green. Green is the color of determination and resistance. This is what boosts your confidence.

2

Self-confidence is a huge power. It gives you the inner freedom to do as much as possible. Whoever believes in himself is always strong and goes far.

3

People who lack self-confidence are not happy. They think they are uninteresting. They doubt their powers.

4

If you are shy, indecisive or withdrawn, this book is for you. After reading, you will definitely become a confident and happy child.

TEST

ANSWER THE FOLLOWING QUESTIONS WITH YES OR NO

1 Do you care what other people think? Are you trying to be good in their eyes?

2 Are you hesitant to do something new? Are you afraid to fail? Are you afraid of what others will say?

3 Do you give up and don't want to continue if something doesn't work out for you? Or do you give up if someone else does the same task better? Do you think you are incapable or worse than the others?

4 Do you have a quiet, inaudible voice? Are you embarrassed to speak in front of your class?

5 When someone asks you a question, do you blush, look away and say nothing? Do you think you won't answer correctly or someone will laugh at your answer?

6 If someone is watching you, do you feel embarrassed and want to become invisible?

7 Do you find it difficult to start a conversation first or to join other children ? Do you get chills at the thought of approaching friends you don't know yet?

8 Can't you or do you find it hard to say "NO"?

If you have at least two **YES** answers read this book carefully, it will help you to be more confident and stronger in your decisions.

This book is designed in an unusual style. Each chapter has its aspect. The reading is very easy and the content is very easy to remember. All colors and playful text are designed with one intention — to grab attention, elicit emotions and capture positive thoughts.

1

What does self-confidence mean?

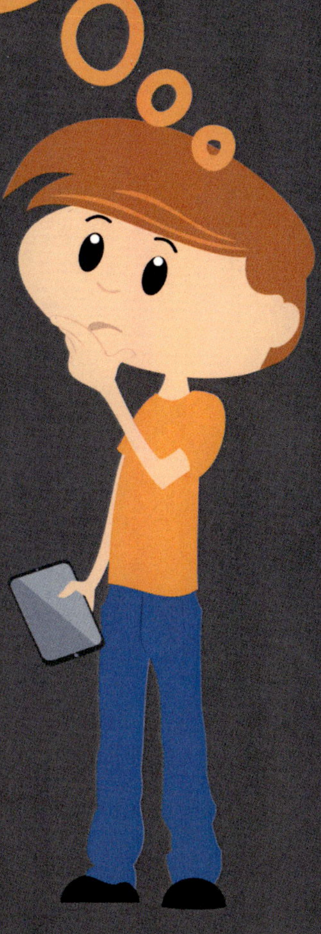

WHAT DOES SELF-CONFIDENCE MEAN ?

THE
SELF-CONFIDENCE

Self-confidence is a power that has a person who understands himself, has beautiful feelings, feels good and treats himself well.

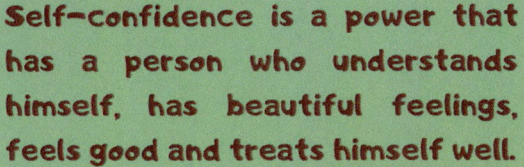

Self-confidence makes a person stronger, so that he does not compare himself to others. He respects himself for his efforts, his courage, even for his failures.

Self-confidence allows you to set goals, believe in yourself and achieve your dreams.

Confidence in yourself allows you to understand your abilities and your limits.

THE LACK OF SELF CONFIDENCE

When someone lacks confidence, they feel fragile. Any rash words can hurt him.

Because of a small problem, life can seem complicated and terrifying, full of difficulties.

EXERCISE

Get up, close your eyes for two minutes. Don't think about anything and look inside yourself. Feel the warmth and beauty of your spirit. Dive into beautiful memories and realize how happy you are capable of being.

Try to feel your inner center. We can call it your "inner world". It grows and grows stronger as you get to know yourself.

Your inner world gradually fills up when you do a lot and understand what you like and dislike in your life. Even when you make mistakes and learn not to make them again, your world grows too.

2

you
are
unique

YOU ARE UNIQUE

Self-confidence gives the feeling that everything is possible and that everything is at your fingertips.

When you are confident in yourself, failures are not perceived as a disaster, but as an opportunity to try again, to do better and to succeed.

For self-confidence to grow, it is important to understand and know yourself well.

I suggest an activity that will allow you to discover what you already know about yourself, but you ignore it.

On the next page you will see what to do.

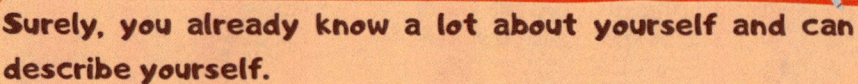

ACTIVITY

Surely, you already know a lot about yourself and can describe yourself.

In a notebook, write what kind of person you are, what qualities you have, what you like, etc. But... wait, you have to do everything in **three steps.**

Attention

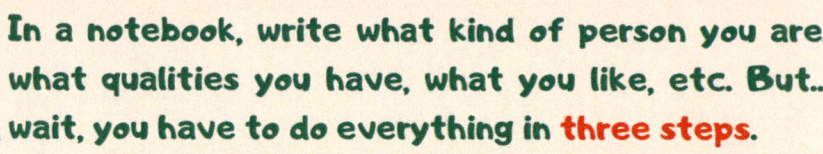

The words "lazy", "indecisive", "capricious", "stupid" are totally inappropriate. These are words that characterize us negatively and condemn us. So forget them!

You have to choose simple and true words that describe you as a person but are not offensive.

words that don't hurt or don't cause harm

Step I — **What kind of person are you?**

Tip

For example, you can write:
"Sometimes I don't know what I want"
"I'm afraid of strangers"
"I love to move and communicate"
"I like to be the first"
"Everything new scares me"
"Often I'm in a bad mood"
"I like when my parents talk to me"
"I don't like it when people don't listen to me"

...CONTINUATION

The more you write about yourself, the better. And remember to review and add to this list when you have time.

You can write 3 sentences about what you think of yourself. Later you can add more.

Take your time to write, for example 10 minutes

Step 2 – What qualities do you have?

Think about your qualities. Those are your strong points.

Choose what you like the most about yourself and write it down in your notebook.

Tip

For example, you can write:

- I keep my promises,
- I am patient, enthusiastic, creative, sociable
- I know how to make my friends laugh,
- I like helping my parents
- I help others.

Think a bit.

You will certainly find qualities in you.

We all have good qualities

Your task, then, is to study yourself, to get in touch with yourself, to note everything that you are doing well.

It is very important to see your strengths, your qualities, your talents and to appreciate them. They give you confidence in yourself.

 **Step 3** – **What can you do best?**
or
What do you like the most?

Find what you can do best and write it down in your notebook.

Tip For example, you can write:

- *I do my homework well*
- *I like drawing*
- *I make beautiful comics*
- *I can do video editing*
- *I can invent stories*
- *I dance every evening*
- *I'm good at math*
- *I like to sing every day*
- *I like to play with my brothers*
- *I prepare my snacks*
- *I like to play with animals*
- *I like taking pictures*
- *I like listening to music*

You certainly know how to do a lot of beautiful activities

WE ALL HAVE UNIQUE TRAITS

- Somebody's got red hair and freckles
- Someone has moles and a bulging nose,
- Someone is tall and hairy,

  - Someone speaks loud and fast,
  - Someone is serious and slow,
  - Someone is quiet and small.

If you have something different from others, there is nothing to be embarrassed about.

You are unique !

There are no perfect people. There is no form of human perfection, because we are all different.

Among the 8 billion inhabitants of our beautiful planet, there is no one who looks like us like two drops of water. Even identical twins are different. Everyone has their own traits, interests, hobbies and dreams.

Never be ashamed of being the person you are, even if you think your ears are big or your voice isn't beautiful, or you're too short. You are unique! It's just beautiful.

Always remember this:

You represent something special, significant and very, very important.

You are a truly unique child — with a unique appearance, qualities and dreams. Earth needed such a boy (such a girl) like you.

 **Keep developing your own interests and hobbies.**

When you do what you really love, your energy and self-confidence grow.
Any hobby is great. None can be considered ridiculous or bad.

Everything you love to do should be developed. This is how you stay true to yourself and fill yourself with energy. Likewise, your self-confidence develops too.

Your emotions are imPORtant

YOUR EMOTIONS ARE IMPORTANT

In you, as in any person, live emotions and different feelings.

It is very useful to know how to recognize them, because your senses always tell the truth. Just listen to them and understand them.

Interesting, can you do it?
Let's check!

1 Imagine you are sitting on the grass and squinting your eyes at the bright sun; it's summer, you're by the pool, you're dreaming and catching the hot rays. And then your mom comes over with a glass of juice and gives you hugs. What are you going to feel?

Of course, joy!

2 Your friend is doing something cool; for example, he (she) tinkers a beautiful picture frame. You stay close and you wait for the result. What is your emotion?

This is interest!

What else?

Curiosity!

Isn't it?

3 The rain is falling, you stay at home, no one calls you. Everything seems to be going well in your life, but something is still wrong. What is this feeling? How do you feel?

Sadness!

4 When a classmate writes in your notebook or throws your pencil case on the floor, how do you feel?

Very probably, irritation and anger.

5 A close friend has suddenly acted towards you in an unexpected and horrific way. What's inside of you in this situation?

There is great confusion and resentment.

You can experience any feeling in your body.
For example:
Pleasure makes you happy
Jealousy makes you furious
Sympathy makes you smile
Horror is blocking you
Nostalgia makes you dream
Hope inspires you

ACTIVITY

Write down in your notebook the situations in which the feelings below appear and grow in you.

FEELINGS	EXAMPLES
Shyness	I am embarrassed to speak in front of my class
Boredom	I get bored when it rains outside
Surprised	I'm surprised when my brother recites poems
Curiosity	I would like to visit other countries
Guilt	I'm sorry that I haven't read any books this week
Pleasure	It feels good to have fun with my brothers
Disappointment	I'm sorry that I did the job poorly.
Courage	I can ride the scariest carousel in the park
Calm	I am calm when I am with my parents
Impatience	I can't wait to go on a trip
Happiness	What a joy to receive many gifts

Now write your sentences using the feelings that are in green.

Continue to next page

...CONTINUATION

FEELINGS   **EXAMPLES**

Respect	I greet when I enter the class
Tiredness	I like to sleep after playing video games
Gratitude	I am thankful to my parents for being by my side
Admiration	The life of my grandparents fills me with happiness
Jealousy	My cousin has more toys than me

Your feelings are neither bad or wrong

All feelings have the same importance, even the most unpleasant.

For example:
- **Fear** is for staying away from something dangerous and not risking your life.

- **Disgust** is for not eating what is bad or poisoning yourself.

- **Anger** allows you to protect yourself and defend what is dear or important to you.

It is impossible to give up unpleasant emotions and have only emotions that bring pleasure.

If you try to "turn off" painful or unpleasant emotions or if you try to hide them, then all emotions will be "disconnected" at once. Yes, yes, all of them.

And then you will not be able to feel either pride, happiness or tenderness.

Without sadness, there will be no joy;
Fearless — not calmness and courage;
Without sorrow — no peace;
Without shame — no self-esteem.

Emotions and feelings are what help you understand yourself and what is going on around you.

All your feelings should be treated with care and caution

Why ?

If you don't pay attention to your fatigue or your sadness, you can get sick.

If you have been angry for a very, very long time you can become very, very angry at the world around you and thus be unhappy.

29

If you pay no attention to your emotions and feelings, if you hide them and lock them up inside you, they will remain trapped inside you and they will cause you a lot of harm.

By ignoring your feelings, you lose touch with yourself, with your inner center.

REMEMBER !

Feelings aren't good or bad. It is normal to feel fear, despair, frustration, embarrassment.

BUT WATCH OUT!

Another thing is the way you express these feelings, that is, your behavior. To be angry and at the same time insult and throw things is not good.

Get angry and talk about your anger with words, without insults, that's good!

Being offended by someone and remaining silent, pursing your lips in the hope that others will notice you and calm you down, is not the best option. You have to say you were offended and ask him not to do this again – that's it!

TIPS

- Always be in touch with yourself, listen to what is going on inside you.

- When you feel an emotion, observe how it behaves in your body and try to name it. For example, if a friend gives you a hug, you feel **affection**. Right?

- If the situation is unpleasant or painful, it is all the more necessary to recognize the emotion that you feel. For example: "I was not allowed to go outside and **I am angry**"; "I said words to a friend that offended him, **I'm ashamed**".

- If you feel an emotion, try to see what it is! Describe what is happening to you, what you are feeling. Your loved ones can help you experience this feeling, for example by telling you: "I'm by your side", "I see that it's hard for you", "You can count on me". **Then you will decide together what to do with the situation that caused this feeling.**

What do I want?

What am I feeling?

How can I encourage myself?

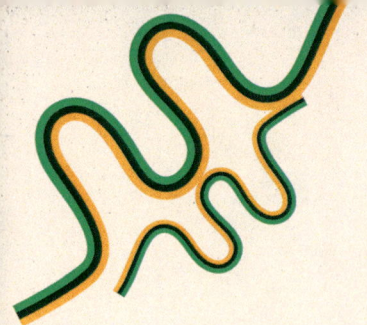

ACTIVITY

Collect in your notebook all the means that help you to live in safety and to face your emotions.

For example:
- stamp my feet and growl furiously if I'm angry
- call a friend and apologize for hurting them
- inhale, hold my breath, and exhale slowly if I'm anxious
- ask for help if I don't know how to proceed
- chew gum if I'm stressed
- take a bike ride if I'm bored
- Close my eyes for 2 minutes if I'm distracted

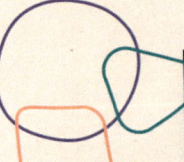

You can add new ways of doing things whenever you think it works for you.

Being able to encourage you in a difficult situation will help you a lot in life.

IT'S A QUESTION OF CONFIDENCE

If you know how to help yourself, nothing will scare you.

Your needs and desires

YOUR NEEDS AND DESIRES

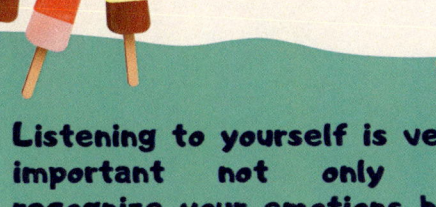

Listening to yourself is very important not only to recognize your emotions but also to feel your wants and needs.

Do you know that desires and needs are two different things?

THE DESIRES ARE NUMEROUS

Surely, you have no problem with your desires. You know what you want every day — a new toy, a treat, more sleep, no homework, etc.

But do you know that your desires are not as simple as you think?

Your desires look like filled chocolates

Desire itself, as you see it in your head, is like chocolate from the outside. In every desire hides an even deeper desire, it is a kind of need or necessity.

THE NEEDS ARE FEW

The needs are different, but in reality they are few in number.

Every desire has a basic need.

Let's take a look at what those needs are!

For example :

– Under the desire to eat something delicious may lie a simple need to eat.

Or maybe it's a need for comfort when you feel lonely and sad and are looking for food to calm you down.

– Under the desire to invite a friend to your home hides the need for communication.

– Under the desire to hug your mother is the need for love.

– Under the desire to be congratulated for your progress in math hides the need for recognition of your efforts.

– Under the desire to be comforted by your parents, after a terrible dream, there is the need for security.

– Under the desire to watch a television program lies the need for relaxation.

It's no shame to need, for example,
- support or to be heard,
- to feel good and useful,
- to be in silence and solitude
- etc

Needs should not be judged. All needs are necessary at some point, and this applies to everyone, not just you.

DESIRES may be good or bad, useful or harmful.

But **NEEDS** are always good and natural.

Your needs must be met so that you can live in comfort and joy, and so that your contact with yourself (your inner world) is not interrupted.

YOUR MOST IMPORTANT NEEDS

1

The need for food, warmth, sleep, bodily contact (hugs).

2

The need to be free of all fear, to be safe.

3

The need for love, acceptance, communication, reassurance, support.

It is very important to feel loved, appreciated and significant.

4

The need for respect, recognition, success.

5

The need to know, to learn, to study.

All to feel capable, talented and respectable.

6

The need for development, achievement, self-expression.

It is important to be yourself, to be different from others and to feel unique.

- **be yourself:** Don't try to please others. Be nice to them, but always have your point of view and express it.

- **be different from others and feel unique:**

Accept all your traits (freckles, big eyes, domed nose, dark skin, flat face, etc). You are beautiful as you were born and you should appreciate yourself for your actions, your feelings and your emotions, not for your exterior. Your inner world is much more important.

You are unique and you make the world more beautiful just by your existence!

ACTIVITY

Try to determine what needs underlie the behaviors or the situations below.

Answer in your notebook, then check the answers by turning the book over (the answer is upside down after each question).

Remember that **NEEDS** are always good and natural!

1

Little Alex is afraid of falling asleep in the dark, he asks his mother to leave the nightlight on. What is the need behind Alex's request?

THE NEED FOR SECURITY

2

Sam thinks only of his new video game that he imagines presenting to his friends. That's why he spends all his free time in front of the computer and creates it. What need compels Sam to take action?

THE NEED TO REALIZE THEIR ABILITIES AND HAVE RECOGNITION

3

Ana and Luca have been friends since daycare. They love spending time together, going for walks and sharing lots of things. A strong friendship is great.
What is the need here?

THE NEED FOR EMOTIONAL CLOSENESS, COMMUNICATION AND SUPPORT

...CONTINUATION

4

Nina was in such a rush to talk about her new friends from school that she fell in the road and hit her knee. She returned home in tears. What is Nina's need?

THE NEED TO BE CONSOLED

5

Classmates sometimes play tricks on Robert because he is fast and often drops things. Robert feels disagreeable, he is offended, even concerned. What need is hidden behind his worries?

THE NEED FOR RESPECT
AND ACCEPTANCE

6

Leya is bored and anxiously awaits Tanya's return from vacation as soon as possible.
What is Leya's need?

THE NEED FOR COMMUNICATION

7

Boris plays with his little brother, he hugs him. Yesterday he even changed his diaper and took him for a walk. What is his need?

THE NEED FOR LOVE AND AFFECTION

know your limits

KNOW YOUR LIMITS

Everyone has their own limits

Do you remember, at the very beginning of the book, I told you about the fact that a person who is confident in himself understands his abilities and his limits. You probably don't know the meaning of the word "limit". But I'll explain it to you now.

For example:
- For health reasons, Michel cannot run all week.
- Maria fails to add two numbers quickly, each time she has to think a lot.
- Denis doesn't like loud music. He is very tired from the noise.
- Marc, after reading a book, almost immediately forgets what it is about.

All these examples speak to us of limits.

 The limit does not make a person bad, incompetent, mean or worse than others.

It is very important to know your limits, without being angry with yourself.

Knowing your limits will allow you to be comfortable and productive.

For example:

- Denis, knowing his peculiarity, can go to his friends, who like to listen to loud music, but spend no more than an hour there; so as not to get tired and at the same time not to lose his friends.
- Marc, in order not to forget anything, after reading his book, must take small notes during the reading and reread them as needed.

Now let's do an activity that will help you to see your limits as a natural thing that you are able to deal with and to have confidence in yourself.

 Limits are frames beyond which a person may not go for any reason.

Thinking you have flaws is no good. It really affects your emotional state and destroys your self-confidence.

ACTIVITY

Remember your limits and write them down in your notebook.

At the same time, think about how to react so that your limits are less felt by you and let you live comfortably.

EXAMPLE:

MY LIMITS:	HOW CAN I HELP MYSELF?
I find it difficult to get up early and be in a good mood.	I prepare my backpack and my school clothes in the evening. Or I go to bed early.

Maybe there's something about you that's hard to accept, something you don't like or your family doesn't like.

For example:
- you have trouble getting along with your friends,
- you count slowly,
- you are afraid of dogs,
- you don't like making new friends,
- etc

What to do in this case?

If you want to have confidence in yourself, you have to reformulate all your limits and turn them into a goal.

For example:
- I can't do the math exercises on my own, which means I have to sign up for math classes.
- I don't know if I like doing anything in particular, so I'm going to try lots of different activities and listen to myself, to find out what I like the most.
- I never get along with my classmates, I will ask my parents to enroll me in a communication course.

We'll talk later about how to move forward, not give up, and achieve what you want.

MINI-ACTIVITY
THE MAGIC CUBE

Draw in your activity book (or notebook) a cube similar to the cube below.
On the sides of the cube, write your three burning desires.

When those wishes come true, you can write down your new dreams.

It feels good to dream and desire something. Our dreams and desires fill us with good energy. They help us understand where to go and what to aspire to.

If you cannot achieve some of your desires yourself, you can always ask for help from your relatives.

They will certainly help you or tell you why they are unable to do so at the moment and what they can offer you in return.

Not all desires can come true overnight.

It may take time. Most of the time it takes patience and effort to get what you want.

6

The self doubt

THE
SELF DOUBT

We have already talked about what builds confidence in you. It is very important to accept your characteristics without criticizing yourself. And know how to appreciate everything you do.

But do you know that there are certain things that make your self-confidence melt away and decrease? What is it, in your opinion?

It's your fears

You and I already know that fear is no shame

Sometimes there are fears inside of you that keep you from expressing yourself freely.

You must not let them "eat" you.

Sometimes it can be scary for you to start something new. Right?

Why ? What are you afraid of ?

1 You are afraid of the unknown or/and you are afraid of failing
And then you feel embarrassed. You think the whole planet is pointing the finger at you, and it's the end of the world.

Here I want to tell you that making mistakes and not always succeeding the first time is quite normal! Even superheroes in movies fail, remember?

And what do they do in this case?

They get angry and can be discouraged, but not for long. They remember to have confidence, start over and keep moving forward. Because it's only by trying over and over and putting in the effort, you can get what you want.

2 Perhaps you are afraid of being in front of a large audience (at a party of friends or in front of your class)? Or are you embarrassed and uncomfortable in the presence of other people?
Do you think others will say unpleasant things about you? Or are they going to laugh at you?

What are you afraid of ?

This is the fear of causing a bad reaction in others. And the fear of feeling like some kind of "not like that" — an unattractive, incapable person.

3 Maybe it's hard for you to start a conversation or ask for help.
Why ?

- You worry that others won't talk to you or that you'll be pushed away.
- You care a lot about what other people think of you.
- You are afraid that someone will judge you, or that someone will point out your weaknesses.

This fear is very insidious and MUST be tackled

Do you know why?

Because it makes you think those around you are better than you and they have a right to judge you.

You shouldn't think that anyone has a right to more than you. Because it will greatly weaken you and deprive you of self-confidence.

You have your opinions and they are as important as the opinions of others.

Of course, people around you can make an impression on you, they have the right to think something of you.

But the most important thing is not what others think of you, but what you think of yourself!

If you consider yourself an intelligent, kind and capable child, then that's fine. You are like that. If you think it's wrong to offend others, to ridicule them — you're right. You must have respect for yourself and for others.

Never forget that:
Everyone has the same human value

No doubt there are children bigger than you, there are those who know and can do more than you. Someone has more financial possibilities, someone always has 100% in their school report.

It's wrong to think that someone is better than you.

Conversely, thinking that you are better than someone who is smaller, weaker or slower is also unacceptable.

You shouldn't divide people into the good and the bad. Because everyone on this planet is so valuable.

Everyone is important!

You too !

... And self-confidence will add value to your existence.

7

I
respect
you
...
you too

I have a secret for you! Even adults don't know about it. This is a secret related to the world around you!

To feel good about yourself, to have confidence in yourself, you have to see a lot of good and attractive things in others.

Don't judge people!

- Give feedback without being asked
- Give an opinion on what does not concern you
- Criticize

Do you know why?

Once you decide not to judge others, you stop judging yourself as well.

In this way, you no longer feel inferior or superior to others.

You begin to feel that you are an interesting and talented person with your own opinions and the same human value.

If you don't judge and condemn others, you will make yourself understood and accepted.

In other words, you will have confidence in yourself!

ACTIVITY

Write in your notebook the good, attractive and interesting things you see in your friends.

- What are their qualities, their merits?
- What can we admire there?

For example, you can write:
- Marc, from my class, has good grades and always helps me with math.
- Chris, my neighborhood neighbor, is very fast. He always wins the race
- Lena, the neighbor behind my house, makes pretty bouquets of flowers.

> Look for all the positives in your friends.
> Don't focus on the wrong things.
> Find out what's good about them.

This activity will help you to accept the way of being of your friends and of yourself.

ATTENTION

Accepting doesn't mean you can't keep growing and improving.

You always need to work on your way of thinking, acting and moving forward.

> When you realize that you have to appreciate and respect who you are, you will have confidence in yourself.

Sometimes boys and girls think that confidence is walking around in the air, giving orders to others, looking down on them and still believing that they are better.

NO !

 Having confidence does **NOT** mean:

- be arrogant
- be humiliating
- look down on others

To have confidence MEANS:

- be happy with oneself
- respect oneself
- respect others

Do you know what that means?

It simply means that you are attentive to yourself, your feelings and your needs.

Dso you know that:

- you have a value
- you are unique
- you are important

Likewise, you must see the people around you: unique, incomparable and precious.

Yes, there are certainly bad guys around you, but in this book we are talking about people who are more or less close to you; the people you know or a little less (friends, neighbours, cousins, relatives, acquaintances). Harmful people should be avoided.

These people don't play a role in your life. So, no need to put them in your way.

Let's return to the subject !

You already know that everyone has their own

- feelings
- needs
- thoughts
- tastes

Everyone has their inner world which is as important to them as yours is to you.

No one is worse or better, superior or inferior

Your desires, your aspirations, your interests are very important.

Respect your choices, but also respect the choices of others!

8

The attitude toward yourself

THE ATTITUDE TOWARD YOURSELF

One of the secrets to self-confidence is to believe in yourself. Believe in your abilities, never compare yourself to others and think well of yourself.

Your parents and relatives can help you a lot.

They should believe in you and support you, see all you are capable of and even congratulate you on your small successes. Thus, you will grow up with self-confidence and a free person.

You have to appreciate yourself

If you doubt your worth, if you are often unhappy with yourself, you find it difficult to treat yourself well.

You must think well of yourself

Instead of thinking:

"I'm stupid and a loser."

You must be thinking:

"Yes, at the moment I'm not doing as well as I would like. I have to put in some effort, understand and try to do better next time."

Instead of thinking:

"Nobody likes me, nobody wants to be friends with me."

You must be thinking:

"I know for sure that I am a rather interesting person, I can be a good friend and I will surely find someone who will like me."

Instead of thinking:

"Nobody liked my photo on the social media page, it's probably because I'm mediocre."

You must be thinking:

"It's my photo, I took it with heart in the park, and I like it very much."

Make sure to turn negative thoughts about yourself into positive, kind and encouraging thoughts, so your self-confidence will only grow.

Never forget:

You can fail in something, you can doubt the success of some of your actions.

This is completely normal.

You may fail and not know everything in the world, but this **DON'T MAKE YOURSELF A BAD PERSON.**

If something isn't working for you or you make a mistake, don't berate yourself.

↳ don't blame yourself

Everybody makes mistakes

SELF-CONFIDENCE MOTTO

- I made a mistake? — So I'm going to fix it!
- Something went wrong? — It doesn't make me bad or incompetent. I'll do my best to make it work next time.

I can! I'll succeed!

These words are magic. They give you a lot of strength and courage to get where you want.

A good attitude towards yourself? It can be learnt !

1 Your qualities, your knowledge and your intelligence — look how many you have. These are your powers, your wealth, your everything.

Everyone has their own powers

You should not compare your power with another person's. You should compare yourself to yourself only. It's the only way to succeed!

For example:
- Yesterday you didn't know how to write, but today you do.
- Yesterday you didn't know what a school is, today you know it.

2 Your power belongs to you! You can increase it as much as you want. The more you learn, the more you know — the more powerful you become.

Be proud of your successes and accomplishments

⚠️ Keep growing to learn new things.

If you work hard, if you make an effort, if you do your best, you will see results and you will have joy. It boosts your confidence.

3 Do more of what you love to do. Because it will make you feel that you are talented and you will succeed.

Do what makes you feel good

⚠️ Always try new things.

When you do something you weren't confident enough to do before — that's very brave of you.

4 A good attitude towards yourself DOES NOT mean that you can do anything.

You must respect yourself, but respect others too

⚠️ Everything you do should be safe and good for you. You must behave in such a way that you are not ashamed of your actions.

For example: Don't insult your parents, your teacher or your friends.

↳ do not offend

5 Sure, it's great if your loved ones congratulate you on your accomplishments, but that's not even the most important thing.

Congratulate yourself for your efforts!

⚠️ It is very, very necessary to congratulate yourself on the work you have done!

For example:

You made a drawing, you understood the math homework — immediately congratulate yourself.

Tell yourself: I feel good! I am Bravo!

➤ From these small but very important daily victories comes self-confidence.

6 Appreciate everything you have, all your abilities, everything you possess. Because it is yours.

Learn to appreciate and respect yourself!

⚠️ Respect yourself for your efforts to learn, to try new things. Respect yourself for your courage.

And even if you don't succeed the first time, you have to try again.

7 You must take responsibility for your own actions.

You are responsible for everything you do

 **If something didn't work for you, it's not anyone else's fault.**

Often a child will say, for example:

- "I got a bad grade. It's not me who learned badly, it's the teacher who doesn't like me."
- "I went outside my neighborhood. It was not me who wanted, but my friends who persuaded me."

Everyone is responsible for their own actions.

- If you got a bad grade, it's because you haven't worked/studied enough.
- If you went beyond your neighborhood when you went out to play, it's because you wanted to. Your friends are responsible for what they do, and you are responsible for what you do.

Why is it important to be responsible for your actions?

1) **WHEN you are RESPONSIBLE for your actions, you are not responsible for the emotions of others. So you don't have to feel GUILTY towards others.**

This means, for example, that:

- if you didn't push someone, you don't have to apologize for their knee pain;
- If you haven't said mean words to your friend, you don't have to explain if he (she) is sad.

 You can certainly help or comfort someone if they need it, but if you're not responsible for their condition, you don't have to feel guilty.

2) WHEN you are RESPONSIBLE for your actions, it also allows you to admit your wrongdoings or mistakes and correct them.

Apologize to those you may have unintentionally offended.

 without wanting

 Making mistakes is natural, but you have to know how to correct them or not repeat them again

For example:

- I'm sorry I didn't bring you the book, I completely forgot.
- I apologize for not calling you yesterday as promised. I went out to play and didn't see the time pass.
- I'm sorry I got mad at you yesterday. I thought you took my notebook.

8 Don't let anyone treat you badly or rudely. If someone uses words that hurt you, it's not because they have the right. No no! It's because he's uneducated, overly spoiled, or just plain dishonest.

You must be able – if necessary – to defend yourself!

If someone treats you badly, says hurtful words, makes fun of you, it's very dangerous for you and your self-esteem (or your self-confidence).

If you let someone be mean to you, your self-confidence will decrease until they turn into a little animal – weak and shy.

No one should humiliate you or hurt you. Don't cry in front of anyone, but take a step forward and ask them why they let themselves talk like that.

You must stand firm and say, for example:
- "Say what you want, I know who I am and how I am. Your mean words don't interest me."
- "Think about what you say, then speak. I have my opinion, and if you don't like anything about me, look at yourself first."

In order to avoid the quarrel leaves the place.

9

Respond without fear

RESPOND WITHOUT FEAR

"Your nose is a little weird. Did you fall off the top?"

"Your eyes are cross-eyed. Were you born like this?"

"Your face is flattened. Did you hit a wall?"

Unfortunately, many people – especially children – are unable to communicate without hurting someone.

Sometimes other people's words hurt a lot, and you feel like something is wrong with you. You think you're not as good or cool as other people.

Because of this, your self-esteem and self-confidence may drop.

So that no one hurts you with "strong" words you must understand that everyone on the planet has the same human value.

Nobody can tell you that you're no good or "not like that" if you haven't done anything wrong to that person.

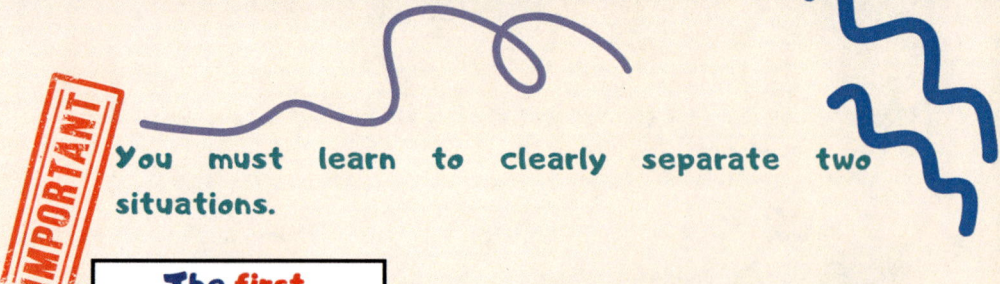

You must learn to clearly separate two situations.

The first situation

You may be causing someone discomfort in some way, but unintentionally.

For example:

- by accident, you stepped on someone's foot;
- you broke without wanting something
- you forgot to keep your promise
- you did not follow an instruction

If similar situations happen to you, it is very important not to immediately feel bad or react with anger.

You must:
- recognize the disturbance caused,
- excuse yourself

and, if possible
- compensate for damage

Give something in return

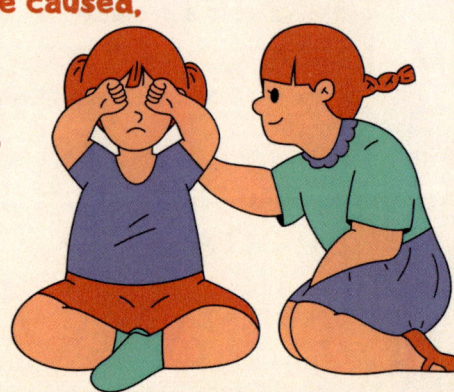

72

Someone, without your asking, starts talking about you with someone else or even ridiculing you.

This is unacceptable!

Rude comments are disrespectful.

An educated person should never say what they think of someone else unless they are asked questions. In both cases, it is necessary to be polite and not to hurt others.

If you hear someone talking badly about you, you don't have to feel bad.

Remember that this is disrespectful and it is not acceptable to talk to people like this.

1)  Sometimes children communicate quite rudely with each other and their words can hurt.

For example:
- "You don't understand anything! Sit down and shut up!"
- "Nobody told you to talk!"
- "What are you doing here? No one called you!"
- "What are you looking at? Get out of here!"

Nobody likes to hear that!

If you have already heard similar phrases, know that it is a usual situation. These children want to prove that you are not part of their group.

Yes, it's hurtful, but you have to understand that these kind of friends are not your level.

You are not better, but you are more educated!

So simply don't accept them.

You don't need friends like that!

You will certainly find friends who know what respect is.

2)  There are worse situations. When children start insulting you, teasing you or making fun of you. You may think these children are very brave and confident, but they are not.

A confident and self-assured person will **never tease** or **make fun** of others.

 A person, who is insecure about himself, actually sees himself as small and unsightly. And in order to feel big and strong, she begins to put others down.

When someone says hurtful words to you, remember that you have to protect yourself.

You can say, for example:

- "You can't talk like that! It's really unpleasant to see how you ridicule yourself by saying that."
- "You're talking nonsense! Think before you speak."

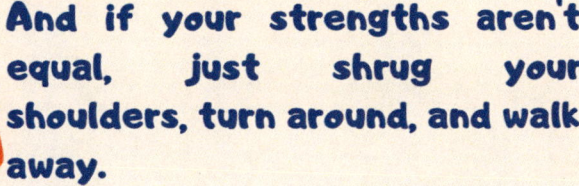

And if your strengths aren't equal, just shrug your shoulders, turn around, and walk away.

For example: if they are several or they are older or bigger than you.

Remember that everything said has nothing to do with you.

These kids just want to hurt you.

The decision not to enter into conflict and not to give in to provocations is a sign of confidence in yourself.

You will certainly find friends who know what respect is.

3)  In life, there are very serious situations. When children don't just say something hurtful, but are really cruel.

They start chasing a person and making fun of him: insulting, humiliating, threatening, ignoring, throwing, hiding and damaging his things, pushing hard, kicking, hitting.

That's violence!

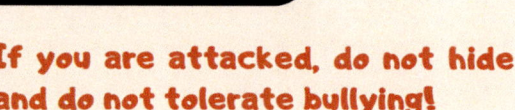

Violence destroys both those who attack and those who are attacked!

If you are attacked, do not hide and do not tolerate bullying!

 Seek immediate help and protection from adults, teachers or parents.

Nobody has the right to humiliate or make fun of others.

Any physical or psychological aggression is absolutely unacceptable.

It is the duty of adults to intervene to stop the violence. Impossible to do it without their help! Adults know that violence in children looks like an illness that needs to be treated urgently.

Even if another child is being bullied, whether you know or don't know, don't shut up.

Go see an adult without waiting!

4)  If you have a page on social networks (Facebook, Instagram, Twitter, TikTok, Discord, etc.), you can easily face attacks there. Someone may insult you or start bullying you. It's very dangerous !

On the Internet, it is difficult to understand who you are interacting with. You may not know who is the one who wants to hurt you.

 It is very important to tell your parents

 Immediately stop communicating with this person and block them.

If you don't know how, ask your parents for help.

 **Any kind of violence is**
ABSOLUTELY UNACCEPTABLE!

GOOD communication
makes life
more beautiful.

- reciprocal
- shared

Mutual **RESPECT**
makes any activity
wonderful.

Each moment spent in
JOY
extends our life.

10

overcome obstacles and achieve goals

OVERCOME OBSTACLES AND ACHIEVE GOALS

EVERYTHING IS POSSIBLE

For you to be confident in yourself, you must understand that you can influence your life and achieve what you want.

do something to change it

But without doing anything nothing happens!

You can, of course, stay and do nothing for a long time or dream that you are a cool and strong kid.

Only in fairy tales, by doing nothing, you become strong and you have everything.

In real life, it's different!

To become **STRONG** (from within of course), you have to read lots of books, learn lots of new things, and participate in activities that make you happy.

And in order for all your wishes to come true, you have to make the necessary efforts.

Remember, even if you don't get what you want on the first try, you're likely to get it on the second try.

For example:

- you want to get a soccer medal
- you want to have the first place in mathematics.

It all depends on your level of preparation and effort.

When you learn new things and try to make interesting changes in your life, it makes you a strong, capable, and confident person.

Also, to have confidence in yourself, you must have goals!

Have goals, is to be happy!

Goals can be easy to achieve, but more often than not, they don't happen overnight.

You should know that things don't always turn out the way you want them to.

So, you may be disappointed not to have the right result immediately.
And that is normal.

Everyone goes through this, but it's important to be prepared so you don't lose your confidence.

 Do you remember the motto of a confident person?

It didn't work, I'll try again!

Your goals must be realistic!

If you try and try but nothing works, think about the feasibility of what you are looking for.

Maybe you just need to simplify the task a little or better prepare yourself to get the result.

Sometimes it's good to take small steps. These small steps can take you far.

Do you know that nobody becomes a doctor, a champion or a computer scientist in the blink of an eye?

Every person we look up to has a long and difficult story of success.

Any Olympic champion who has won a gold medal will tell you that he has been preparing and training since childhood — long and hard.

All the effort and love you put into an activity can lead you to a great and joyful victory.

Before setting a goal, you must decide:

- **What do you want exactly?**
(for example: finish your school year with high marks, play the piano, finish designing a video game, read a hundred books in a year)

- **How long does it take you to reach the goal?**

- **Is your goal achievable given the time and resources at your disposal? (Do you have everything you need to achieve your goal?)**

You already know that unexpected obstacles can arise while you are on your way to your goal.
But you should never give up, because there is always the possibility of reviewing your strategy (and making changes if necessary).

ACTIVITY

Write in your activity book what your goals are.

What do you want to accomplish, succeed or become?

For example :
- Have lots of medals
- Have a dual screen computer
- Not wanting to eat a lot of sweets
- enjoy physical activities

So your goals are set. You just have to reach them.
And to help you, the next chapter will be very useful.

11

The action plan

THE
ACTION PLAN

To achieve your goals, you must make an action plan.

The action plan is a preparation or an organization before achieving an activity or a goal.

1) TRY

Of course, you have to try to do (or want) something that you want to know or learn.

It must be something you like or are interested in.

If you succeeded, congratulations!

If you weren't able to achieve your goals, move on to the next point.

For example, you wanted to have a computer, you did all your homework well during the year, you followed your parents' advice. So you got a reward for Christmas: a computer.

! If something goes wrong, you'll know what to do to the next point.

2) THINK

Something went wrong? Give yourself time to recover.

You may be angry or sad, but don't let this go on forever.

You need to think about what went wrong.

Did you manage to achieve part of your goal?

For each small success, you should congratulate yourself!

3) START

Start with something small, something you like or something you already know how to do.

What you have achieved once causes special pleasure and a desire to do the same again.

Find what you can learn quickly and easily in your new activity.

And get to work; don't let this drag on for another time.

When you enjoy the fact that you receive something in return for the work done, you will have the desire to continue and get where you want.

For example, you want to win first place or at least second place in swimming.

You know that you are already good at this sport, but you haven't yet participated in competitions between several schools.

You understand that to get the place you want, you have to make an effort. You have to work before the competition.

You use various techniques to practice swimming speed, you train with the friends of your group.

So you're looking for what's easy and quick to do. Just dedicate more time to training and you're done.

4) ASK

For your activities, your projects, you can always ask for help.

You can choose someone to teach you what you haven't learned yet.

Who can this person be?

Mother, father, grandmother, grandfather, brother, sister, friend or other person who knows the task or has more experience than you.

Don't be shy and don't hesitate to ask for help.

Together it's always more fun and easier.

Strong support from loved ones works wonders.

The person helping you should not do the work for you. Let her encourage and support you.

And if you don't know how to do something, ask him to tell you or show you how to do it.

But it's up to you to make the effort, to try and finally get what you want.

It's now your turn to make an action plan to succeed.

On the next page, a little activity awaits you.

ACTIVITY

In your notebook, make your action plan that will allow you to succeed in what you want to do.

Also write the names of people who can help you.

YOUR ACTION PLAN:

MY WAY TO REACH AN OBJECTIVE	THE PEOPLE WHO WILL HELP ME
First I... For example, I want to create a video game First I will read a book on creating video games or watch on You tube.	Father Cousin George (he's an IT worker) Uncle Ben (he has a lot of computers)
And if that doesn't work, then I... If I don't quite understand, I will sign up for online classes or activities.	Father Mom
And then ... I like to build various things from wooden blocks. I could make an electronic construction game. I have a computer, now I need to check what I need to do to be able to create a game.	Uncle Ben Cousin George Mom Father

It may take a lot longer than expected to achieve a goal. It all depends on what you choose. When you get to where you wanted, you will have a sea of joy and pride.

These feelings strengthen your inner world. If you always try and overcome various obstacles, you will no longer be afraid of difficulties or of doing something new.

If you succeeded once, you will succeed again. Because you're already prepared, you know what it takes to get there — put in the effort!

All this makes you internally free and sure of yourself.

12

I have confidence in myself !

I HAVE CONFIDENCE IN MYSELF !

I have confidence in myself, because:

1) I accept myself as I am!

2) I treat myself and I think well of myself!

3) I trust my emotions and my needs!

4) I explore, I recognize and I accept my capacities and my limits!

5) I am responsible for my actions!

6) I pay attention to my behavior and I am wary of others' judgments!

7) I respect myself and I respect others!

8) I'm happy with my successes and I don't underestimate my accomplishments!

9) I set realistic goals and strive to achieve them!

10) I recognize my errors and my bad deeds; I am not looking for excuses, but I am trying to correct them!

11) I learn from my mistakes. And I try not to commit them again!

12) I know it's natural to have doubts. It is impossible to succeed in everything and always!

13) I don't blame myself when I fail!
Failure is a reason to revise my tasks and do things better.

14) I appreciate my effort and patience, even if something doesn't work for me!

15) I don't compare myself to others!

16) I'm not afraid to speak!

17) I don't intentionally hurt anyone and I expect others to do the same!

18) I can ask someone I know for help!

19) I have the right to say "NO" to what does not suit me!

20) I start to keep a diary of my achievements that I call: "My successes"!

If you trust yourself, others will trust you too!

Self-confidence is
the courage
to be yourself!

CONTENTS

Made in the USA
Las Vegas, NV
05 December 2022

61202815R00059